WINDOWS 10

FOR SENIORS

2020 User Guide to Master Microsoft Windows 10
with Updated Tips and Tricks

Tech Treck

Table of Contents

Chapter 1

Introduction

Thank you for making the right choice to buy this book and welcome to the magnificent world of the Microsoft Windows 10 operating system. This book has a lot of information you might not be able to find elsewhere. It has been designed so you can build your skills as a beginner.

Microsoft Windows 10 has been around for a while and there are several updates that have been released.

This book is specially written for the following persons;

- Those who have become frustrated with Mac OS or other boring operating systems.
- Those who have just upgraded from an older operating system.
- Those who recently purchased a new computer with Windows 10 already pre-installed.

This beginner's guide will take you on a tour of Microsoft Windows 10 to get you started with using the operating system. You will also learn how to perform tasks and Windows 10 user settings. The steps are presented in a simple format to make you have a wonderful learning experience from one page to another.

In this book, we will go over the basic layout and learn how to perform certain tasks and later dive deep into the Windows 10 settings menu.

So, this is a beginner's guide intended for brand new users to the operating system to learn the absolute basics. If you are a power user, you can get the intermediate or advance version from the same author.

Windows 10 Installation

There are more than one Windows 10 installation methods: You either carry out an upgrade from your previous Windows or you do a clean installation.

When you carry out an upgrade on your operating system, you will still have all your installed applications and documents intact.

A clean installation option will require you to erase your hard drive to start from scratch. This option is mostly recommended in case your hard drive has issues.

Windows 10 operating system has its minimum system requirement which include:

- A 1GHz processor
  - RAM size of between 1 to 2GB but Microsoft recommends 4GB.
  - A dedicated hard drive space of 6GB.
  - Above all, during installation, the process will scan through your system to determine if it is suitable for a Windows 10 upgrade or installation.

Chapter 2

Getting Started with Windows 10

The Desktop

When you turn on your computer with Windows 10 installed, you will see the lock screen. Just right-click the mouse or press any button on the keyboard to unlock, or choose a user account and enter your password. If it is your computer and you are the sole user, simply click on your name and enter your password to unlock the screen.

It is very important to have your desktop protected with a password, so you don't have anyone having a free ride into your system.

Once you have signed in, the first interface on your computer is the desktop.

The Desktop

Your desktop layout may look different, it is the main workspace of your computer, and it is where you manage and access your files, open applications installed on your computer, access the internet, and a whole lot more. You have the main window (the area with a picture) and a bar covering the bottom of your screen.

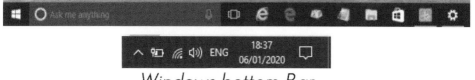

Windows bottom Bar

The bar at the bottom has the following features;

The Start Button

The *Start Button* at the far bottom-left has the same icon as Windows 10 (with four white rectangles).

Start Button

The Cortana Bar

Next beside the start button is the *Cortana bar.* Depending on your Windows settings, if the Cortana bar is active, you will see an 'O' shape with a Mic icon.

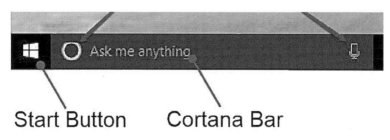

Start Button   Cortana Bar

If your Windows does not support the Cortana bar, you will have the Search bar in its place.

The Search bar also shares the same spot with the Cortana bar. When activated, you will see the 'O' icon beside the search bar.

Cortana is Microsoft's digital assistant and can be best described as a combination of Google Now and Apple Siri.

Cortana provided information when you ask for it and gets better the more you continue to use it. When activated, Cortana can alert you of incoming meetings, help you search the web and your computer, inform you about weather, news and major sports briefings.

To look for an item, type in the word on the search bar and it will display results of your request and reads them to you with Cortana.

Typing can be a bit of a hassle, probably another best way to activate Cortana is by using your voice. You can just say 'Hey Cortana" and it will activate instantly.

For example, I typed in the word "Kindle", the search bar immediately displays content on my computer that has the search word.

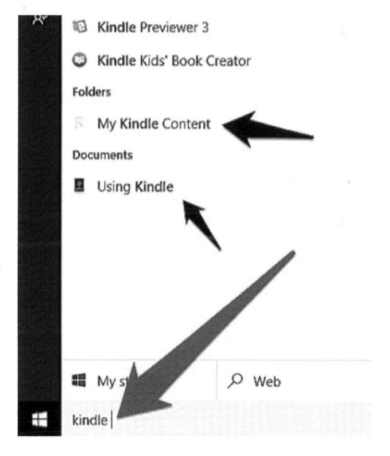

Another way to use Cortana is by clicking on the microphone icon and then use the word "Hey" followed by the "Cortana" to ask your questions.

So, for example, if I click on the microphone icon, next I use the word "Hey Cortana" followed by my question "what is the weather in New York City right now"

Cortana will browse the internet to search for answers to your question. Your computer has to be connected to the internet for this to work.

You can get a copy of my book on how to use the voice assistant and questions you can ask Cortana.

The Task View

Next beside the Cortana bar/ Search bar is the *Task View*. It is a small icon that looks like an open book.

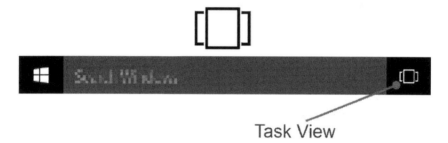

Task View

Task View was originally designed to make it easier to see and switch quickly between running applications.

However, the feature has been evolving ever since it was first introduced, and now, you can also resume activities you were working in the past, as well as use virtual desktops to organize related tasks.

Task View effect on Windows

The TaskBar

Next beside the task view is the *Taskbar*. The taskbar stretches wide towards the left of your screen.

Task Bar

Start Button   Cortana Bar   Task View

The taskbar is an element of Windows 10 operating system located at the bottom of the screen. It allows you to locate and launch programs through Start and the Start menu, or view any program that is currently open.

The Notification Area

The Notification Area is located next after the Taskbar. It shows different types of notifications from your computer, such as your Internet connection, battery level, volume level, language option, etc.

At first, the Notification Area shows a limited amount of icons. But you can click the upward arrow on its left-side to see other icons as well.

Chapter 3

Windows 10 Start Menu

The Start button has been part of Windows from Windows 95 all the way up to Windows 7. When Windows 8 was introduced, Microsoft removed the "Start Button" completely. It replaced the "Start Button" with the "Start Screen". Users complained so much that Microsoft returned the "Start Button" but not the functionality.

When you click on the *Start button,* you have access to the *Start Menu.* The start menu is a hybrid of the Windows 7 Start Menu and the Windows 8 Start Screen. The Start menu grants you access to all the applications on your computer.

There are two main methods to open the Start menu;
    1. Using the mouse to click on the Start Button.

Start Button

2. By tapping the Windows key on your Keyboard.

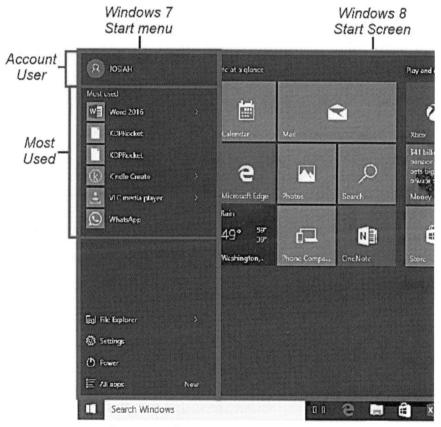

The Windows 10 Start Menu

On the left of the Windows 10 Start Menu, you have the Windows 7 style Start Menu.

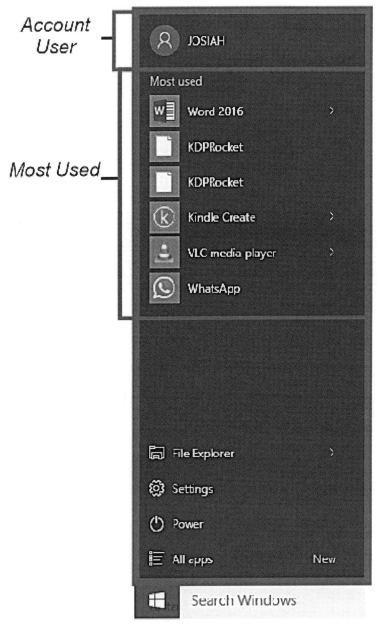

Windows 7 Style Start Menu.

The middle section shows the "Most used" and recently installed applications on your computer. These items can be applications you recently made use of with their respective icons to help you easily identify them at a glance.

Most Used __

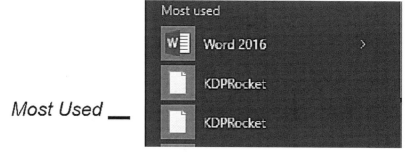

When you use your mouse to right-click on an application you recently used, you will be able to view the files associated with that application usage.

Resizing the Start Menu

You can also resize the start menu to make it narrow or wide as you did like.

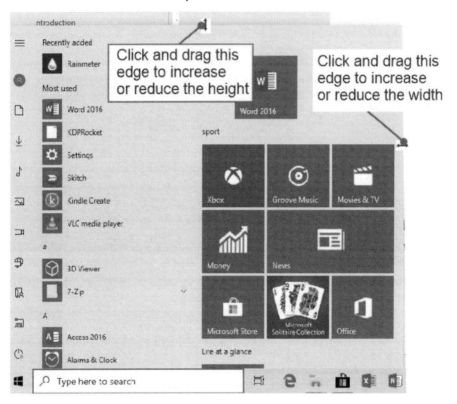

All Apps Access

When it comes to viewing all the applications installed on your computer, one way is to use the all apps option under the start menu. To see all the apps installed on your computer, use your mouse to Left-click on *All apps.*

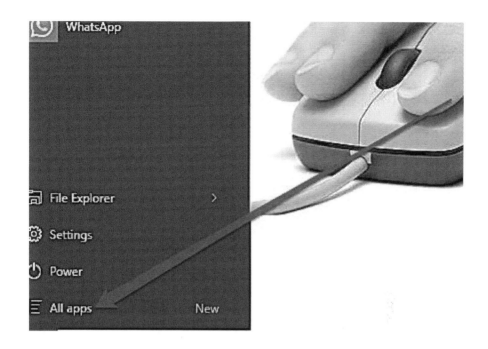

Once you click on *All apps,* Windows will present you with an alphabetical list of all the applications installed on your system. *All Apps* in the Windows operating system are the list of applications that are pre-installed as default within the Windows and the application added by you.

On the right of the list is the scroll bar and scroll button. Scrolling to the correct application is as simple as looking for the app alphabetically. When you find what you are looking for, simply click on it and run that application.

The more application you have, the further you will scroll. To go back to the default Start Menu, click on the *Back* button.

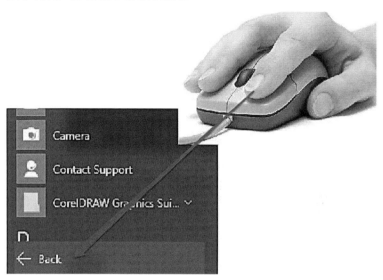

Some of the entries have a *drop-down arrow*.

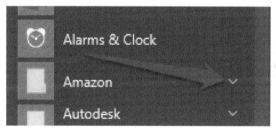

These are folders that contain additional apps that will expand when clicked.

Another method to find an application is by selecting a letter from the All apps.

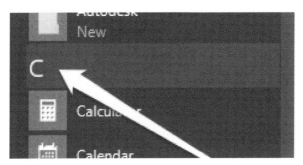

For example, I clicked on the letter C, this will pop out alphabets from A - Z, including symbols and numbers for me to click on the First letter that starts with the name of the app I want to jump to.

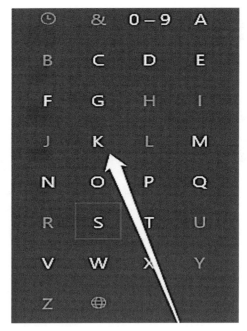

When I click on the letter K, all the apps on my computer starting with the letter K will appear.

Tiles

At the right pane, you have a varied array of Tiles similar to what was in Windows 8. These tiles are movable; you can drag and drop them in another spot by clicking and holding the mouse button.

Windows 10 Tiles

Tiles are basically shortcuts to apps available in the Microsoft Store, you should not confuse them with regular Start Menu shortcuts for desktop apps like Google Chrome, Firefox, Adobe Reader, and others. They can be designed to display information in real-time from the applications they point to.

Unlike regular shortcuts, tiles can display information without you having to open the apps they point to. For example, the Weather app displays detailed information about the weather forecast.

The information that your tile displays can be presented in various forms, depending on how the tile is designed, ranging from simple text to an image or even a set of images.

The News app, for instance, sequentially displays trending news. Tiles that are set to live, rotates between text and photos.

To make a tile aminate and toggles between different sets of information, you right-click on the tile using your mouse and select Turn live tile on.

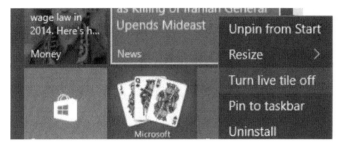

If you don't like a flashy and distracting amination on a tile, you can turn it off, by right-clicking and select Turn live tile off. This will make the tile to become static and only display the name and logo of the app. To manage the amount of space taken by tiles on your screen, you can change individual tile sizes. The app tiles can usually be Small, Medium, Wide and Large in sizes.

Shortcuts tiles only come in Small and Medium sizes. To see the available sizes, right-click the tile, or tap and hold (if you have a touchscreen) and then access the Resize menu.

To remove a tile or shortcut from your Start Menu, you right-click on it and select the Unpin option.

To rename a tile or group, double click on the title and replace the name to that of your choice.

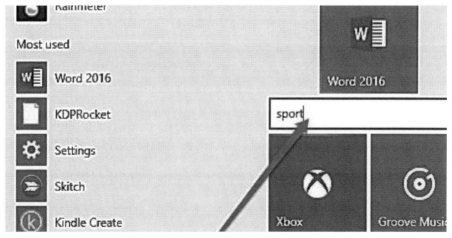

File Explorer

The File Explorer is the file management app used by the Microsoft Windows operating system to browse through the files and folders on your computer. See it as a digital filing cabinet.

There are two main methods you can use to access the File Explorer.

1. By using the Start Menu.
2. By using the File Explorer icon in the Taskbar.

The start menu option gives you additional features to work with, by clicking on the white drop-down arrow.

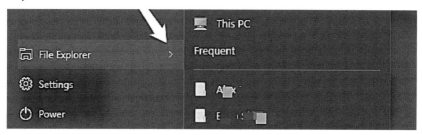

The File Explorer callout menu under the Start menu shows you *"Pinned"* and *"Frequent"* categories. From here, you can explore specific folders on your computer.

The *Frequent* section changes dynamically, showing you the folders you most commonly open on your computer. More about File Explorer and File Management will be discussed in chapter 5.

Settings

Being able to change the settings that govern the way your computer or device works is important in any operating system. Windows 10 is no different, and its settings app continues to receive new updates, making it easier than ever to find a setting and to set up everything according to your preferences.

Microsoft is gradually phasing out what used to be its Windows control panel. The Settings app under the Start Menu is more simplified and easy to use.

A lot of settings have been moved to the new interface. So there is a single user experience across desktops, tablets, laptops, and phones.

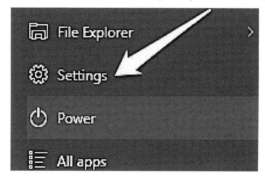

To access the *Settings* app, click on the Start Menu, then select Settings. But for a previous Windows user who prefers to use the old "Control Panel", or need a feature not available in the new Settings app, you can go through the *Quick Access Menu*. To access the Quick Access Menu requires you to right-click on the Start button.

This will display the quick access menu list with the control panel option for you to click on.

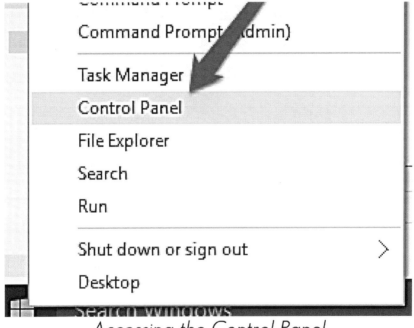

Accessing the Control Panel

Windows Settings

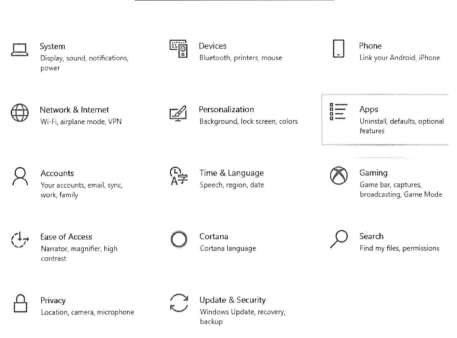

The November 2019 update Windows Settings

If you are using the older version of Microsoft Windows 10, you might not have access to all the features. The following are categories under the Settings app:

System

Display, sound, notifications, power

- *System* - settings that let you change the display and sound options, configure notifications and manage power options.

Devices
Bluetooth, printers, mouse

- *Devices* - settings that give you control over the devices connected to your computer, including Bluetooth devices, printers, scanners, the mouse, and the keyboard.

Phone
Link your Android, iPhone

- *Phone* - settings that give you access to the content on your mobile device.

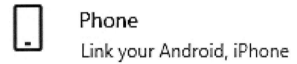

Network & Internet
Wi-Fi, airplane mode, VPN

- *Network & Internet* - settings that allow you to configure your ethernet and wireless adapters, proxies, VPN, and everything related to the way you connect to the Internet.

Personalization

Background, lock screen, colors

- *Personalization* - settings that let you customize Windows 10's overall look, including colors used, Background, Lock screen, Themes, Taskbar, and Start Menu.

Apps

Uninstall, defaults, optional features

- *Apps* - settings related to the apps available on your Windows 10 computer or device.

Accounts

Your accounts, email, sync, work, family

- *Accounts* - settings that control the accounts used on your Windows 10 computer or device, sign-in options, and syncing.

Time & Language
Speech, region, date

- *Time & Language* - settings that let you change the date, time, region, language, and speech options.

Gaming
Game bar, captures, broadcasting, Game Mode

- *Gaming* - settings that control your gaming experience and how you share it with others.

Ease of Access
Narrator, magnifier, high contrast

- *Ease of Access* - settings that are meant to enhance or change the way you interact with your Windows 10 computer or device.

Search

Find my files, permissions

- *Search* - settings that let you modify how Windows 10 searches for files.

Cortana

Cortana language

- *Cortana* - settings that control Cortana, Windows 10's version of a virtual assistant.

Privacy

Location, camera, microphone

- *Privacy* - settings that let you control permissions for Windows 10 and apps, including the information they can access and use.

Update & Security
Windows Update, recovery, backup

- *Update & Security* - settings that manage Windows 10 updates, as well as backup and recovery options.

Microsoft did its best to organize the Settings app, a search feature was also added to the Settings app.

Windows Settings

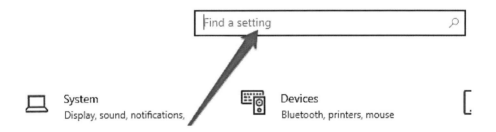

Find a setting 🔎

System
Display, sound, notifications,

Devices
Bluetooth, printers, mouse

When opening Settings, a large "*Find a setting*" field is displayed at the top, in the middle of the window. Start typing keywords for the setting you are looking for inside the "Find a setting" field. The Settings app will suggest matching settings, which you can click on, to take you straight to it.

The Power Buttons

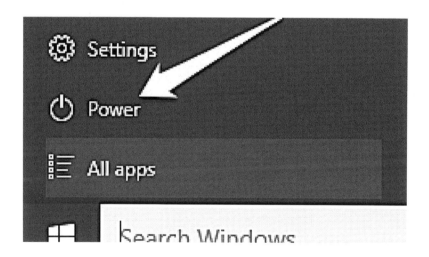

When you click on the power button, additional options will pop-out, which includes *Sleep, Shut down* and *Restart.*

- *Sleep* puts your computer in a low-power state so you can quickly resume where you left off. All your running applications will be right where you left them once you wake up your computer from sleep. It uses less battery, but not as much as when it is turned on. Once you press a key or move your mouse, it will wake up as long as you are not having issues with Sleep Mode.

- *Shut Down* closes all your open programs, shuts down the Windows, and then turns off your computer. Since it's completely shut off, you can unplug the power cord from your computer.

- *Restart* shuts down Windows and your computer, then starts them back up again. You will often have to restart after installing or uninstalling software or updates, and it fixes all kinds of issues too.

Chapter 4

Windows 10 Personalization

Whether you want to have a darker color scheme, run several apps at the same time, or display multiple desktops, Windows 10 allows you to personalize your PC in cool ways. It gives you the power to make your computer look exactly how you want it.

The lastest version of Windows 10 comes preloaded with exciting cool features to customize your desktop background, and a variety of settings to modify your Windows interface. In this chapter, I will walk you through steps to customize your Windows appearance and make it a little more personal.

How to Rename Your Windows 10 Computer

1. Go to Settings

2. Select System

3. Click on About

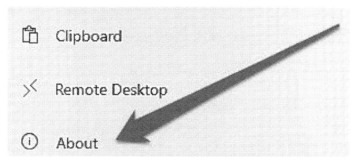

4. Click on *Rename this PC* button

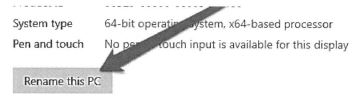

5. Enter the name of your choice in the box and click on Next, then restart your PC to complete the process.

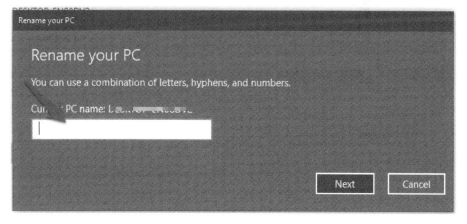

How to Make the Start Menu look Bigger or Broader

To change between the default and full-screen Start screen, go to the Settings app under the start menu. Click on Personalization, and click Start. Next, toggle on *Use Start full screen*. Then click the Start button to see how it looks like.

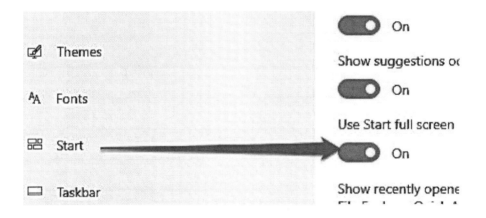

As you can see below, the start menu covers the entire screen on my device shown below.

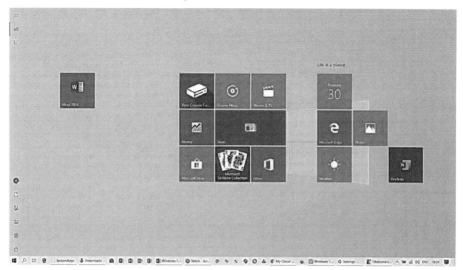

This setting is also useful when you don't want anyone to see what you were initially doing. It is also useful for users with impaired vision and likes to see the menu items in a bigger size. We shall go further to look at more start menu settings you can carry out and its effect.

How to Display more Tiles on the Start Menu

Go to *Settings› Personalization› Click on Start›*
Toggle on the *Show more tiles on Start* option.

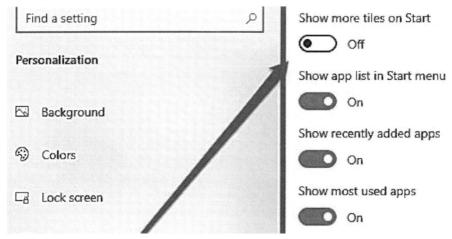

How to Display Or Hide App lists on the Start Menu

Go to Settings› Personalization› Click on Start›
Toggle on the *Show more tiles on Start* option.

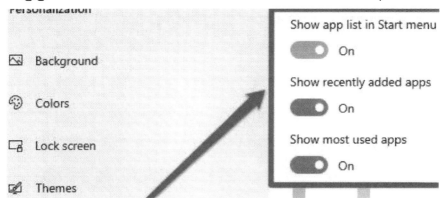

How to Show app list in Start menu

Show app list in Start menu

 On

This displays or hides the list of applications installed on your computer to choose from when you click on the start menu.

How to Show recently added apps

Show recently added apps

 On

This displays or hides the list of applications recently installed on your computer.

How to Show most-used apps

Show most used apps

 On

This displays or hides the list of applications mostly used on your computer. So you can quickly access such apps without having to search for them from the list.

How to Display Or Hide suggestions on Start Menu

To make it easier for users to know about new apps, Microsoft store app place suggestion for apps and games on the start menu to lure users to install on their system.

If you consider these suggestions as a distraction and wish to disable it, you can do this by following these steps.

Goto to the Settings app under the start menu> click on Personalization > Click on Start.

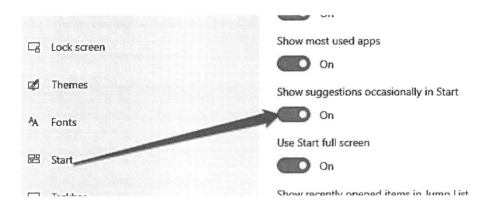

Click on the button to toggle button to turn it Off. If you wish to see these ads again, follow the same steps to activate it.

How to Change your Desktop Background

Changing the desktop background with a custom image or collection of images is one of the simplest ways to add some personality to your desktop. You can even add new themes by using pictures from your gallery.

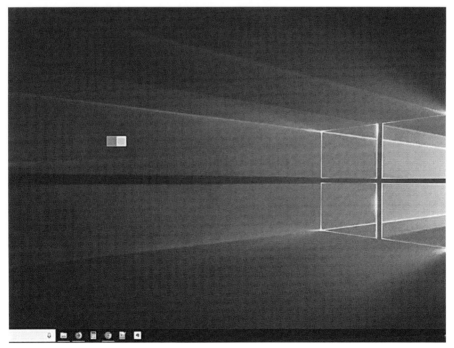

To change your desktop background;

1. Click on the Start button, and select *Settings.*

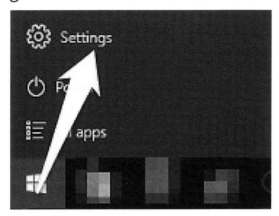

2. Click on *Personalization.*

3. Click on *Background.*

4. Using the "*Background*" drop-down menu, select the Picture option.

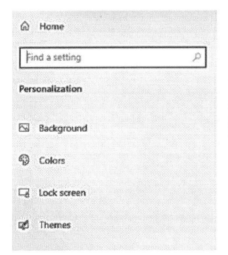

Background

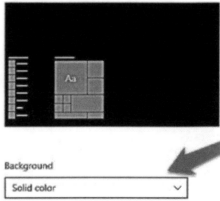

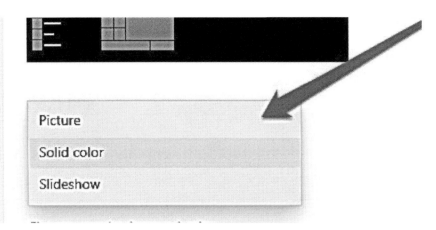

Picture

Solid color

Slideshow

5. You can choose pictures presented to you or click on the *Browse* button to select your own personal image (probably that of your kid or loved one) to use.

Choose your picture

Browse

6. Using the "*Choose a fit*" drop-down menu, select the option that best suits the image, including fill, stretch, center, span, etc.

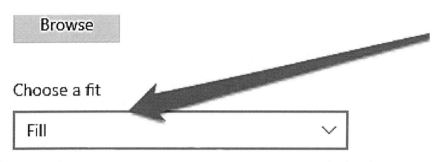

Choose a fit

If you choose to use a picture or a slideshow as your desktop background, you can decide which position you want the image to be or look like on your screen.

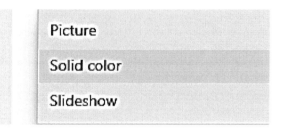

The options available;

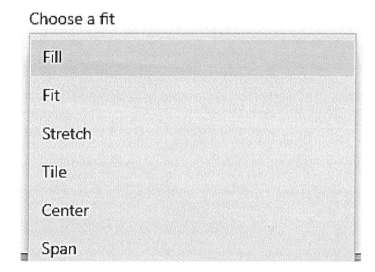

- *Fill-* this places the image at the center of your screen. The images fill the screen both horizontally and vertically yet maintaining its original aspect ratio. In some cases, some portion of the image overrun the edges of your screen either horizontally or vertically.

- *Fit-* This places the image at the center of your screen. The image occupies your screen horizontally or vertically still maintaining its original aspect ratio. Some portion of the image might not occupy the horizontal or vertical edges of your screen.

- *Stretch-* this places the image at the center of the screen, filling the screen horizontally and vertically. When you make use of the stretch option, the image won't maintain its original aspect ratio and does not overruns your screen.

- *Tile* – with this option selected, the image is fixed at the upper-left corner of your screen maintaining its original size but will be duplicated as much as possible to fill your entire screen.

- *Center*- The image is placed at the center of your screen maintaining its original size.

- *Span* – This option is useful when making use of multiple monitors connections. With this option, you can stretch the image selected across all the monitors connected to your computer.

How to Set up Background on Multiple-Monitor

Additional monitors allow you to expand your desktop, getting more screen real estate for your open programs. Windows makes it very easy to set up additional monitors, and your computer probably has the necessary ports.

Setting a unique background on each of your multiple monitors was a simple trick in Windows 8, but the option is buried to the point of being invisible in Windows 10. To change desktop backgrounds individually for each monitor, go to Settings › Personalization › Background.

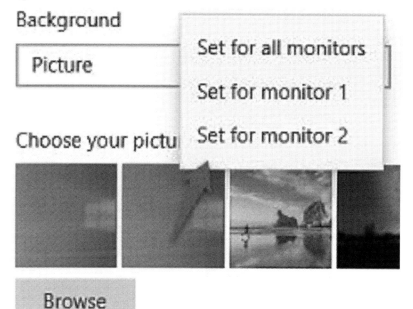

Under Choose Your Picture, right-click a background image and select "Set for monitor 1," "Set for monitor 2," or whichever other monitors you want to use it on.

Choose your picture

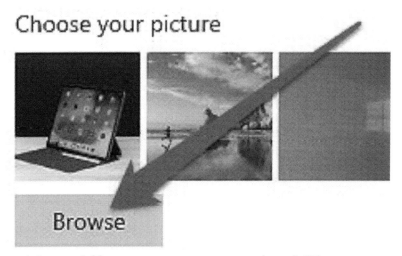

Browse

To add a different image to the "Choose your picture" list, click on the "Browse" button. Windows will set it as your default on all desktops. Right-click the wallpaper icons and choose which monitor you want to use it.

How to Create Custom Themes and Dark Mode

Windows 10 finally brings control of themes into the Settings app to add a personal touch to your computer. To access themes settings, you follow the same process of going through the start menu, go to *Settings › Personalization › Themes.*

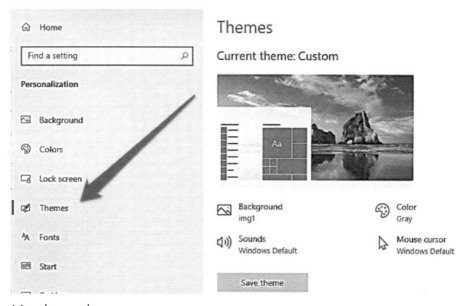

Under these settings, you can create a new custom theme for Windows 10 by changing various aspects like the background, accent color, type of mouse cursor, and sound options. When done, you can save a Windows 10 theme containing all your settings.

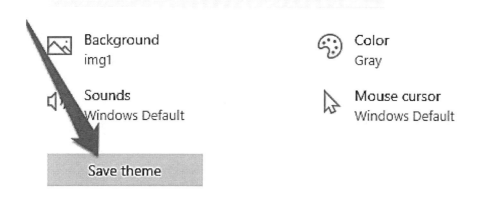

How to Set up a Desktop Slideshow

A desktop slideshow or desktop background slideshow is a handy feature available in Windows 7, Windows 8/8.1 and Windows 10 to automatically shuffle desktop background picture at given intervals. The desktop slideshow feature can be enabled and configured by navigating to the *Start Menu > Settings> Personalization.*

You will have to click on "Background" to continue. Next, use the "Background" drop-down menu to select the *Slideshow* option.

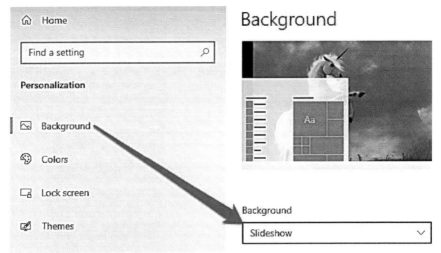

Click the *Browse* button to select the folder were you have the images.

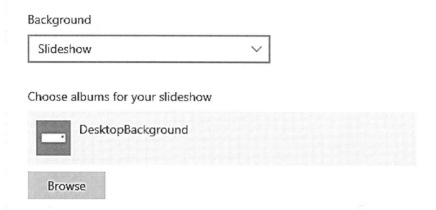

Use the "Change picture every" drop-down menu to select how often you want the image to rotate.

If the order of the images is not important, turn on the Shuffle toggle switch.

Using the "Choose a fit" drop-down menu, select the option that best suits the images, including fill, stretch, center, span, etc.

Alternatively, you can download themes with nice Windows 10 backgrounds in 4K resolution from Microsoft Store. Go to the Start menu> Settings> Personalization> Themes. Scroll down and click on "*Get more themes in Microsoft Store*" option.

To have access to Microsoft Store, you must log in or create a Microsoft account.

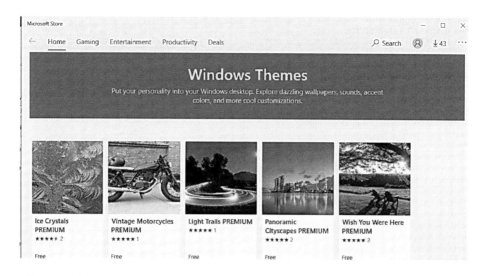

If you have the same Microsoft account logged in on other computers, your downloads and settings will get synced to them as well.

How to Add or Remove Folders on Start Menu

Having your folders placed on the Start menu is another way to have quick access to such a folder(s) once you log into Windows. You can add as much folder as convenient for your Windows screen to display every time you click on the Start menu. To carry out this task;

1. Click on the Start menu.

2. Click on Settings.

3. Click on Personalization.

4. Select Start.

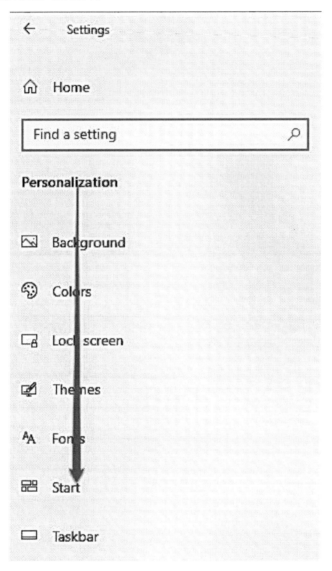

5. On the left side, click on *"Choose which folders appear on Start"*

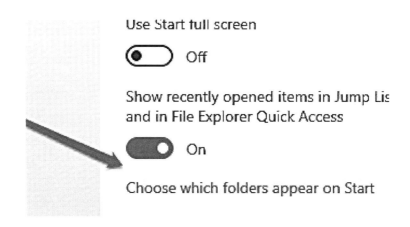

Use Start full screen

Off

Show recently opened items in Jump List and in File Explorer Quick Access

On

Choose which folders appear on Start

6. From the list, toggle ON or OFF any of the options.

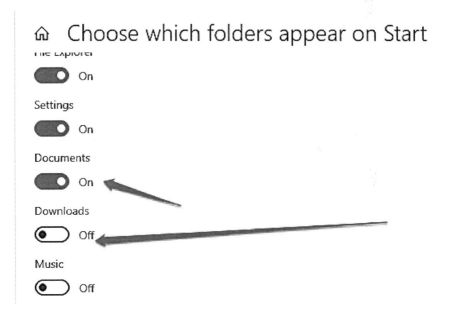

⌂ Choose which folders appear on Start

File Explorer

On

Settings

On

Documents

On

Downloads

Off

Music

Off

For example, I have the Downloads and Music folder turned off from the Stat menu. So once I click on the Start menu, I have really quick access to these items.

Taskbar and Action Center Customization

The taskbar is an element of the Microsoft Windows 10 operating system located at the bottom of the screen.

It allows you to locate and launch programs through Start and the Start menu, or view any program that is currently open. You can also check the date and time, items running in the background through the Notification Area, and with access to the File explorer quick launch. If you are familiar with Apple Mac, think of the taskbar as the Dock.

Two instances of a Microsoft Word Program

When you open a program in Windows 10, the program you are actively on will be highlighted on the taskbar. If you happen to have more than one additional program open in an instance, it will be kind of subtle. You will have to hover over the program icon on the taskbar to see.

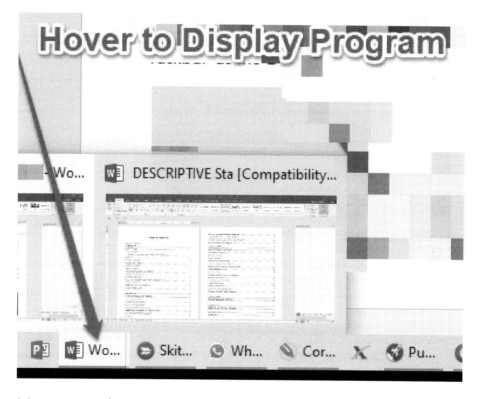

Here you have two instances of Microsoft Word program open, but you have to hover to see the previews and then choose between them.

How to descriptive and separate running program icon on the taskbar

To show individual running program icon without stacking them as one, right-click on the taskbar and select Taskbar settings.

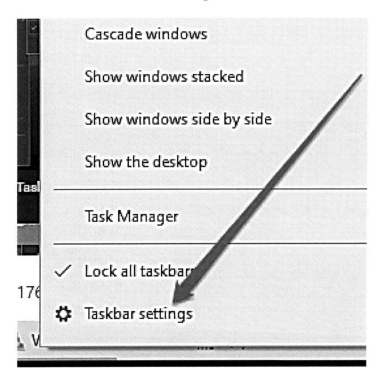

This will take you to the Windows 10 settings apps under the Personalization option.

Depending on your screen size, scroll down or under the combined taskbar buttons options, select *Never*.

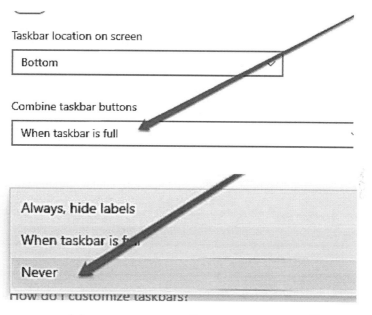

On your taskbar, you will now see all running programs with their icon separated depending on the number of such programs running in an instance. Making it much easier to distinguish between different programs running at an instance.

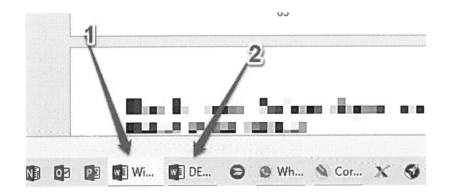

How to make Cortona Appear as a Button on the Taskbar.

This will remove the search box which might be taking up space on the taskbar and make Cortana appear as an icon.

Right-click on the search box/ Cortana, click on Cortana, select Show Cortana Icon.

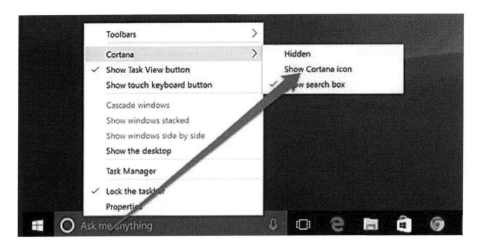

How to Change the Taskbar Color

Black is the default color for windows 10 start menu, taskbar, and the action center. If you don't like the taskbar color, you can change it to suit your taste. This requires you going to the start menu to click on the Settings app. Next, you click on Personalization > then select colors.

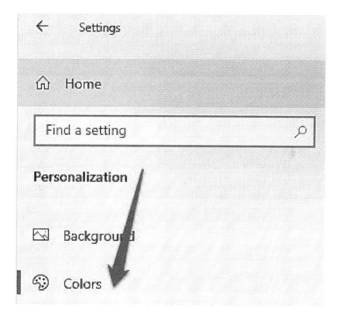

You then choose a color or your personal color by clicking on the Custom color.

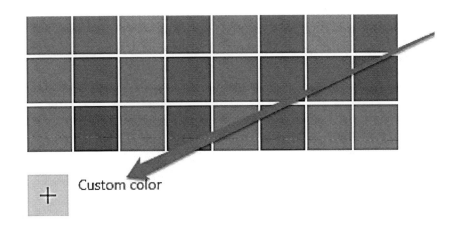

Custom color

Show accent color on the following surfaces

In order to change your taskbar color to match the color on your desktop background, ensure you pick *Automatically pick an accent color from my background* and *Show accent color on Start, taskbar, and action center.*

☑ Automatically pick an accent color from my background

☑ Start, taskbar, and action center

How to change or show default desktop icons in Windows 10

The Windows 10 desktop contains a range of icons, some of which appear when you install Windows 10, and some that appear when you install a new program. Icons with an arrow are known as shortcuts or links to programs, files or folders. You can double-click on a desktop icon to launch that program, folder or file.

Meanwhile, Windows 10 default desktop icons include; Computer, Recycle Bin, User's Files, Control Panel and Network.

Desktop default icons are designed to enable quick access to frequently-used programs, files, folders and so on. To change or display windows 10 default desktop icons,

1. Go to Settings under the start menu and click on Personalization > select Themes> Click on Desktop icon settings.

Personalization

Background, lock screen, colors

Related Settings

Desktop icon settings

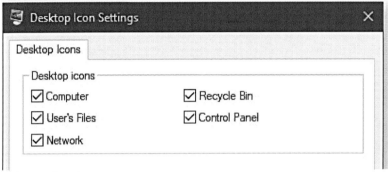

Pick which icons you want to appear on the desktop, and then click OK.

Chapter 5

File Explorer and File Management

File Explorer is the Windows 10 operating system's file management application used to browse folders and files.

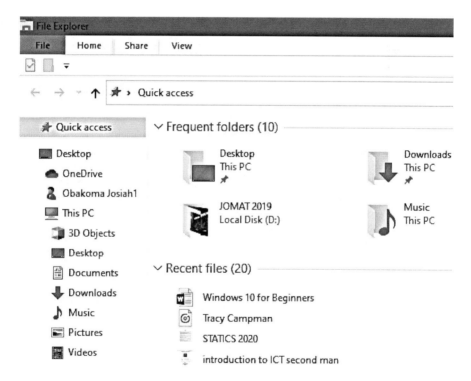

The file explorer's interface allows you to navigate and have easy access to files stored on your computer.

To access the File Explorer through the *TaskBar,* you will have to click on the File Explorer icon.

The location of the File Explorer on your taskbar does not matter, just look for a yellow icon with a light-blue rectangle at its bottom.

Windows 10 File Explorer makes things easier when searching for your files. When you launch File Explorer in Microsoft Windows 10, you get access to the Quick access window.

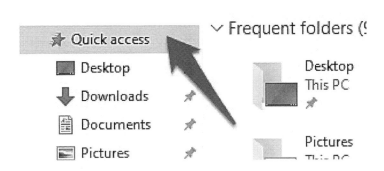

Formally, the Quick access windows were referred to as *Favorites* in previous versions of Microsoft Windows operating systems; here in Windows 10, you will see your most frequently accessed folders and files you created.

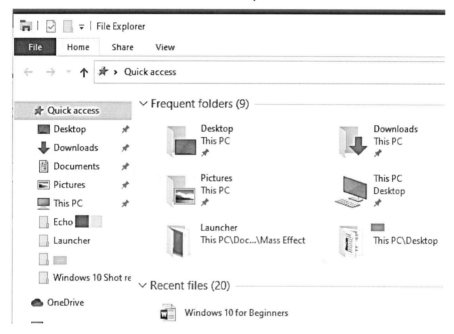

To access contents under the Quick Access column, you only have to click once.

Other areas such as under the *Frequent Folders* in the File Explorer require you to double click on an item to open it.

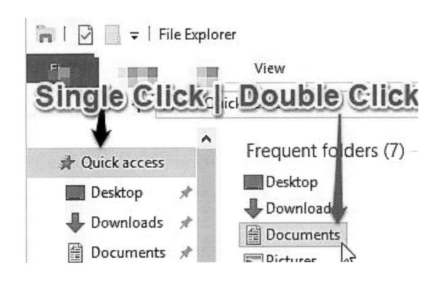

File Explorer Ribbon

The file explorer ribbon allows you to carry out common tasks, such as copying and moving, creating new folders, emailing and zipping items, and changing the view. The tabs change to show extra tasks that apply to the selected item.

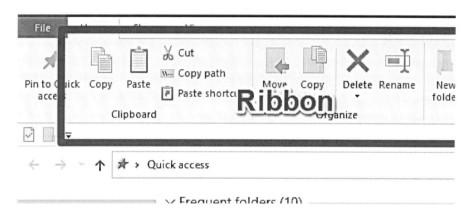

The Windows 10 file explorer ribbon has four tabs, each with its own different commands.

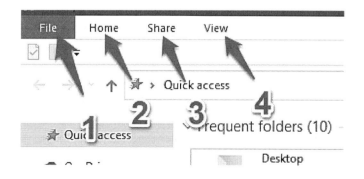

On the *Home Ribbon,* you have the features below.

Mostly used commands on the Home Ribbon include;

- Copy- used in copying a file of folder

- Paste – used in relocating or create a duplicate after copying a file or folder

- Copy Path- used in copying the path of a file or a folder.

- Copy to- used in copying a file or a folder to a specific location.

- Delete- used in deleting a file or a folder from your computer to the recycling bin. and pasting files and folders from one place to another.

- Rename- used in renaming an existing file or a folder

- Property- this allows you to check the property of a particular file or folder. One of the information mostly looked for here is the size of the file and file path.

On the *Share Ribbon,* you have the features below.

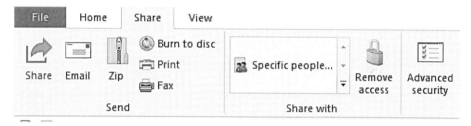

Mostly used commands on the Share Ribbon include;

- Share- used in sharing a file or a folder with a nearby device using your Bluetooth or wireless connection.

- Email- used in sending a file or folder using Microsoft outlook. You will need to add a Microsoft outlook profile in order to make use of this feature.

- Zip- used in compressing a folder so as to reduce its actual size.

On the *View Ribbon,* you have the features below.

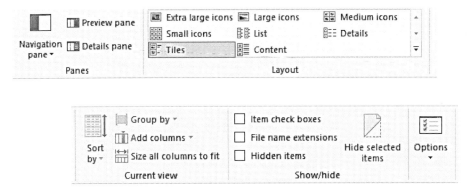

Mostly used commands on the View Ribbon include;

Show or hide the Navigation pane in File Explorer

The Navigation pane on the left side of the file explorer interface offers the easiest and fastest way to browse through your files. Not every user likes the idea of having the navigation pane visible on their file explorer interface. You can hide the navigation pane completely or some of its features using the view ribbon.

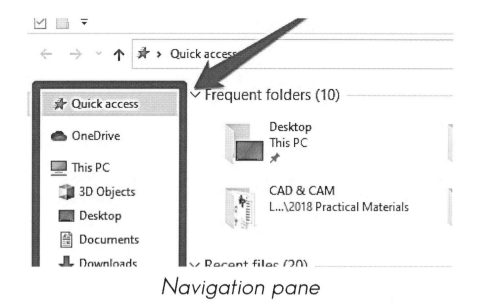

Navigation pane

To modify the look of the navigation pane, click on the View tab, and go to the Navigation Pane section of the View ribbon. Click on the Navigation pane and deselect or select the options to hide or show.

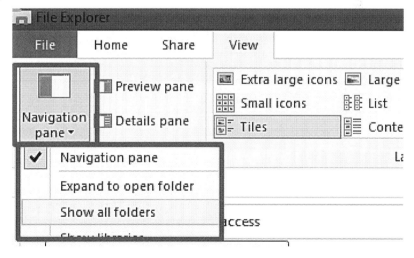

Expand to open a folder

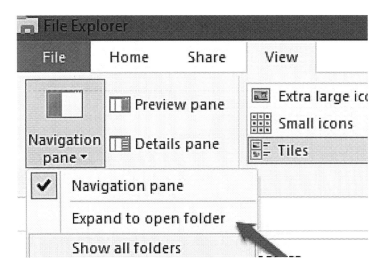

This option enables your folders on the navigation pane to expand as you click on them. If deselected, your folders on the navigation pane will be compressed.

Show all folders

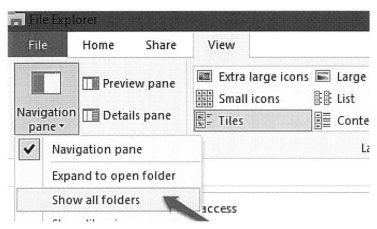

This option allows you to show all folders on your computer in a single group on your navigation pane. If this option is not selected, you will have a more brief folder view arranged into applicable sections like Quick Access, This PC, OneDrive, Control Panel, and Network.

If you deselect the Navigation Pan, it will remove the Navigation Pane from your file explorer interface.

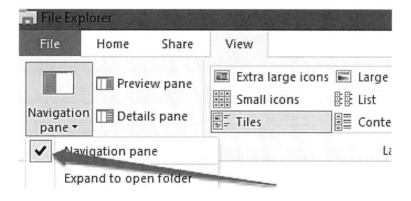

To return the Navigation pane, do the same action.

How to Hide or Show the File Explorer Ribbon

The fastest way to show or hide the file explorer ribbon is by pressing Ctrl + F1 key on your keyboard.

For better files and documents organization, having a group related files into separate folders on your computer will help you easily find what you need.

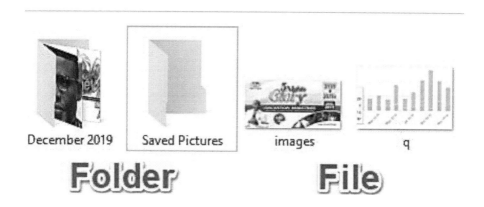

December 2019   Saved Pictures   images   q

Folder   **File**

You can also change the icon size to make it more visible.

Creating Folders

The fastest way to create a new folder in the file explorer interface in Windows 10 is using a combination of keys on your keyboard.

When you are in the spot where you want to create a new folder, press the following combination of shortcut keys on your keyboard

CTRL+Shift+N. Hold down the Ctrl, Shift, and N keys simultaneously.

Below you have an example of a new folder created under my music.

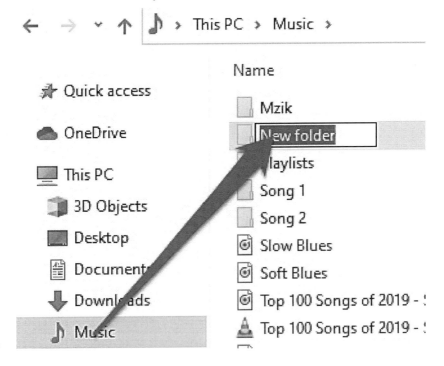

I made use of the *Quick access* panel to click on Music. While in the music folder, I used the shortcut keys on my keyboard CTRL+Shift+N to create a new folder.

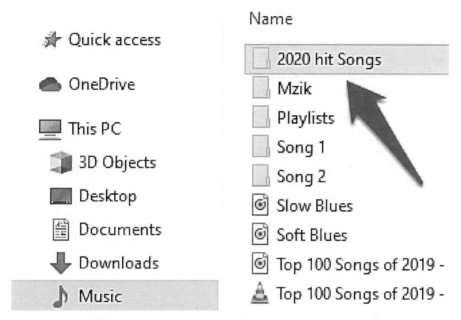

Name

⭐ Quick access

☁ OneDrive

🖥 This PC

   📦 3D Objects

   🖼 Desktop

   📄 Documents

   ⬇ Downloads

   🎵 Music

- 2020 hit Songs
- Mzik
- Playlists
- Song 1
- Song 2
- Slow Blues
- Soft Blues
- Top 100 Songs of 2019 -
- Top 100 Songs of 2019 -

Next, I will have to immediately type or remain it as 2020 hit Songs.

Renaming a Folder

You can also rename an existing folder by simply right-clicking on the folder. Next click on rename and type in the new name you desire for the folder.

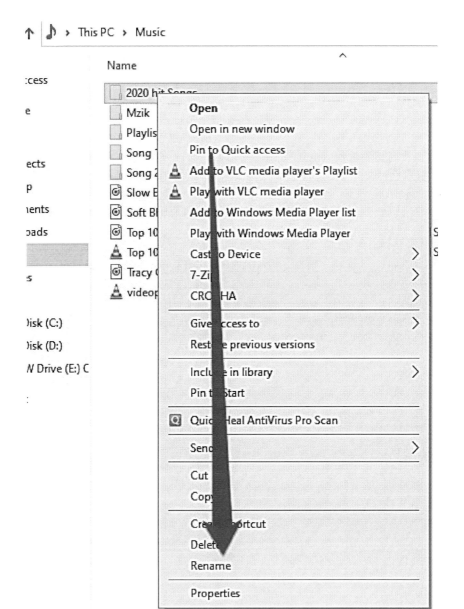

↑ ♪ › This PC › Music

Name ⌄

:cess

e   2020 hit Songs
           Mzik   **Open**
           Playlis   Open in new window
           Song   Pin to Quick access
ects   Song 2   Add to VLC media player's Playlist
p   Slow B   Play with VLC media player
ients   Soft Bl   Add to Windows Media Player list
oads   Top 10   Play with Windows Media Player   S
           Top 10   Cast to Device   >   S
:s   Tracy (7-Zip   >
           videop   CRC HA   >

isk (C:)   Give access to   >
isk (D:)   Restore previous versions
N Drive (E:) C   Include in library   >
                         Pin to Start
:   Quick Heal AntiVirus Pro Scan

                         Send   >

                         Cut
                         Copy

                         Create shortcut
                         Delete
                         Rename

                         Properties

Windows 10 Performance Enhancement

Having a slow computer can be frustrating, but you can try some tips in this chapter to speed up the performance of your Windows 10 computer.

1. In your notification settings, turn off *Get tips, tricks, and suggestions as you use the Windows* option.

   ☑ Show notifications on the lock screen

   ☑ Show reminders and incoming VoIP calls on the lock screen

   ☑ Allow notifications to play sounds

   ☑ Show me the Windows welcome experience after updates an occasionally when I sign in to highlight what's new and sugge

   ☑ Get tips, tricks, and suggestions as you use Windows

2. If your hard drive is filled up with files that you may no longer have use for, having them cleared out of the computer gives your computer a speed boost.

   Go to the Settings app under the start menu and click on Storage option.

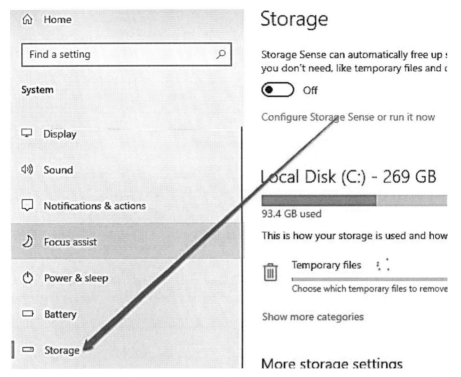

Toggle on Storage Sense to automatically monitor your system and free your storage from files you have no use for, such as the temporary files.

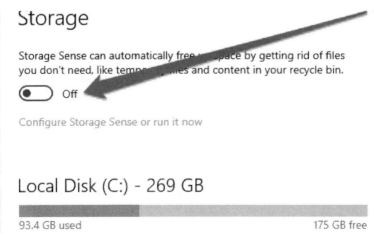

You can go further to determine how often you want the Storage sense to free up space automatically on your computer.

Depending on the Windows 10 version, with the November 2019 release, click on *Configure Storage Sense or Run it Now.*

Storage

Storage Sense can automatically free up space by getting rid of files you don't need, like temporary files and content in your recycle bin.

 On

Configure Storage Sense or run it now

Select the interval at which storage cleaning is to be carried out as you wish.

Storage Sense

 On

Storage Sense runs automatically when you're low on disk space. We cleaned up 4.09 GB of space in the past month.

Run Storage Sense

Every day	∨

How to remove Windows 10 temporary files

Temporary files are commonly referred to as those files stored by apps on your computer to hold information briefly.

Though, Windows 10 has several types of temporary files, including those spare files after installing a new version, error reporting, temporary Windows installation files, upgrade logs, and more.

Normally, these files don't cause any problem, but they can increase in file size quickly, thereby using up valuable space on your computer hard drive and make it slow in performance. Temporary files can also be one of the reasons preventing you from installing a new version of Windows 10.

To instantly remove temporary files on your computer using the Settings app on Windows 10 Version 1909,

1. Open the Settings app

2. Click on System, then select Storage.

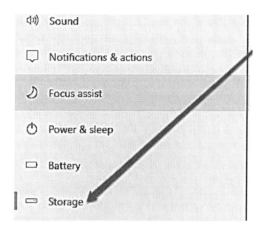

3. Under Local Disk, click on the Temporary Files option.

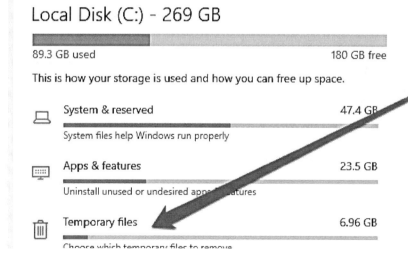

4. After scanning through your system, a list of temporary files will be displayed for you to select from those you want to remove.

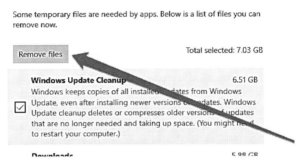

5. When done selecting your temporary files to be removed, click on *Remove Files* button.

Alternatively, using storage sense can automatically free up space by removing those temporary files on your computer.

1. Go to the Settings app
2. Click on System
3. Click on Storage
4. Ensure Storage Sense is toggled On.

In addition, you can click the *Configure Storage Sense or run it now* option to modify the *cleanup settings or run Storage Sense on-demand.*

Set the interval at which you want this process to be carried on.

Temporary Files

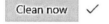 Delete temporary files that my apps aren't using

Delete files in my recycle bin if they have there for over

| 14 days | ∨ |

Delete files in my Downloads folder if they have here for over

| 14 days | ∨ |

Free up space now

If you're low on space, we can try to clean up files now using the settings on this page.

Clean now ✓

Chapter 6

Windows 10 Notifications and Settings

The notification area also referred to as the system tray in Windows 10 is located in the bottom-right corner of your computer screen, where you have the system clock.

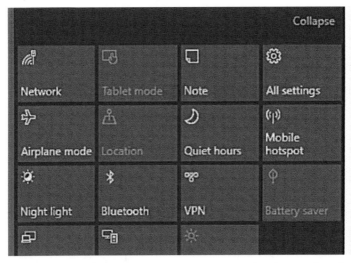

This is the notification action center which gives you quick access to your computer's commonly used settings and notifications.

With an administrative privilege, you can add or remove the notification area on the taskbar.

How to Configure Notification Display Period

To configure the number of seconds that notifications display on the screen in Windows 10;

1. Go to *Settings*
2. Click on *Ease of Access.*

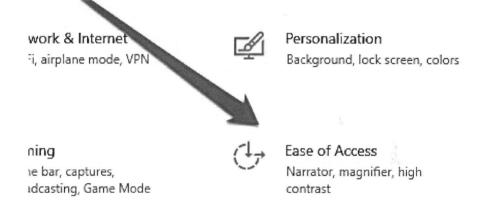

work & Internet
Ϝi, airplane mode, VPN

Personalization
Background, lock screen, colors

ning
ιe bar, captures,
ιdcasting, Game Mode

Ease of Access
Narrator, magnifier, high
contrast

Under simplify and personalize Windows, scroll down and select *Show notification for* to determine how long you want the notifications to show for.

Simplify and personalize Windows

Show animations in Windows

On

Show transparency in Windows

On

Automatically hide scroll bars in Windows

On

Show notifications for

5 seconds ⌄

Show desktop background image

On

You have the option to select from five seconds
or up to five minutes.

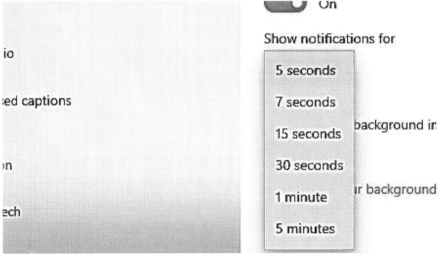

How to Configure Apps that can Display Notification

You can also choose specific apps that can show notifications.

1. Go to Settings
2. Select System
3. Click on Notifications & Actions. And from there you can Toggle On or Off the notifications from each app.

How To Turn Off All Notifications from Apps

1. Go to Settings
2. Select System
3. Click on Notifications & Actions.
4. Toggle Off Get Notification from apps and other senders.

Notifications

Get notification apps and other senders

On

To control times when you do or don't get notifications, try Focus assist.

How to Hide or Show Icons in the Notification Area from Settings

1. Go to Settings, and click on the Personalization icon.

2. From your left, click on Taskbar and click on the *Select which icons appear on the taskbar* link.

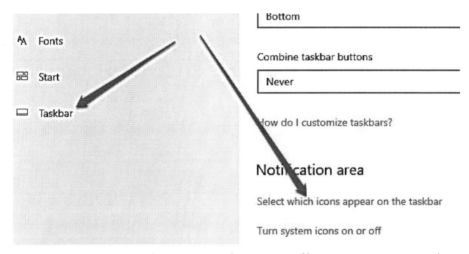

3. Turn on Always show all icons in the notification area and toggle on the sets of notifications you wish to see on your taskbar.

⌂ Select which icons appear on the taskbar

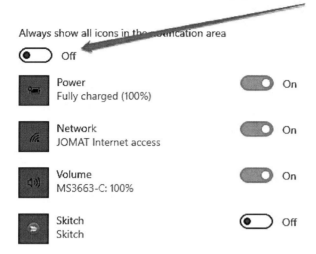

How to Hide or Show Notification on Windows 10 Lock Screen

Notifications automatically appear on the Windows 10 lock screen. This allows you to stay in the loop without having to unlock your device. If you don't want all notifications appearing on the lock screen, you can turn this feature off.

1. Go to the Settings app on the start menu

System

Display, sound, notifications, power

Device

Bluetoc

2. Click on the System option and select notification and actions.

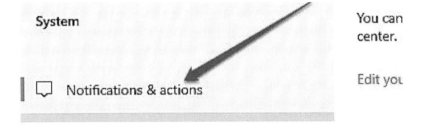

System

You can center.

Notifications & actions

Edit you

3. Toggle off the *Show Notification on the lock screen.*

Chapter 7

Windows 10 Networking and Sharing

In this chapter, you will learn several Windows 10 networking concepts: your workgroup, your computer name, your IP address, your network location, and your Homegroup. My aim is to help you understand what these concepts are as a beginner and the role they play in network sharing.

Workgroup

The workgroup is an assembly of computers that belongs to the same network. These computers are peers and cannot control other computers of the same workgroup. Computers in the same workgroup are easy to detect and able to carry out the sharing of resources like folders or printers.

In order to avoid complications in carrying out file management, Microsoft recommends that no more than 20 computers should be on the same workgroup.

How to Check Your Computer Workgroup

Your computer is part of a workgroup called "WORKGROUP" by default. This allows you to set up your network quickly without the need to carry out any kind of configuration.

To check your system workgroup profile, on your search bar, enter "Control Panel"

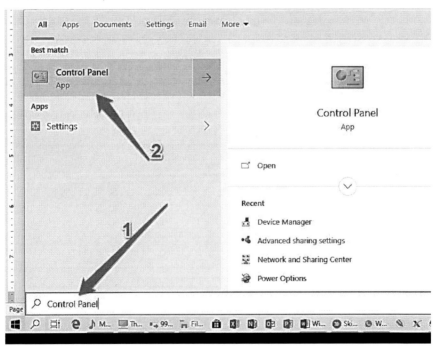

1. From the list click on Control Panel
2. Click on System and Security

Adjust your computer's settings

System and Security
Review your compute... ...atus
Save backup copies of y... ...files with F
Backup and Restore (Wind... ...7)

Network and Internet
View network status and tasks

Hardware and Sound

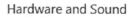

3. Click on systems

Control Panel Home

- **System and Security**
Network and Internet
Hardware and Sound
Programs
User Accounts
Appearance and
Personalization
Clock and Region
Ease of Access

Security and Maintenance
Review your computer's status and
Troubleshoot common computer p

Windows Defender Firewal
Check firewall status │ Allow an a

System
View amoun... ...M and processo
See the name of this c... ...uter

Power Options
Change battery settings │ Change

File History

Look for the entry named "Workgroup".

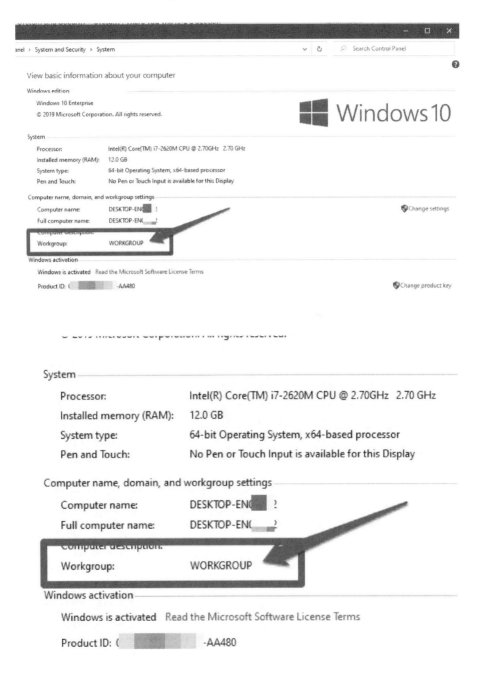

How to Check your Computer Name

During the installation of a Windows operating system, you will be asked to enter your computer name. The computer name is necessary to identify the computer when connected to a network. To check your computer name, use the search bar to go to "Control Panel > click on *System and Security* > then click on *System*". There you will see the name of your computer as illustrated below.

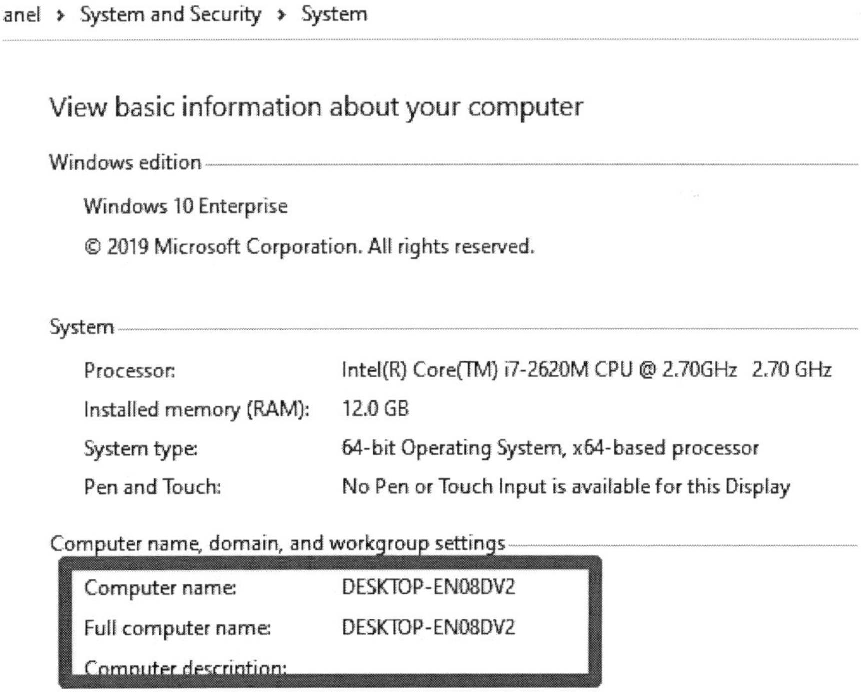

anel › System and Security › System

View basic information about your computer

Windows edition

Windows 10 Enterprise

© 2019 Microsoft Corporation. All rights reserved.

System

Processor:	Intel(R) Core(TM) i7-2620M CPU @ 2.70GHz 2.70 GHz
Installed memory (RAM):	12.0 GB
System type:	64-bit Operating System, x64-based processor
Pen and Touch:	No Pen or Touch Input is available for this Display

Computer name, domain, and workgroup settings

Computer name:	DESKTOP-EN08DV2
Full computer name:	DESKTOP-EN08DV2
Computer description:	

How to Check your Computer IP Address

Your computer IP address means your "internet protocol". These are binary numbers used to identify your computer whenever you are connected to a network. To check your system IP address, on your keyboard press the Windows key and R key to open the Run Window. Type in "cmd" and click on OK.

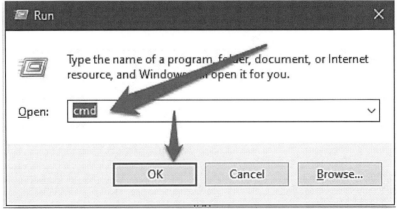

Type in "ipconfig" and press the Enter.

The IPv4 Address displays your computer's IP address.

How to Check your Computer Homegroup

The use of a homegroup is to make the sharing of files and printers among the member of a home network easy. It only works if you are on a home network location. You can only join a Homegroup if your network connection is chosen as home.

To check your computer network location,

1. Go to your system "Control Panel", and click on "Network and Internet.

Aujust your computer's settings

 System and Security
Review your computer's status
Save backup copies of your files with File History
Backup and Restore (Windows 7)

Network and Internet
View network status and tasks

 Hardware and Sound
View devices and printers
Add a device
Adjust commonly used mobility setting

 Programs
Uninstall a program

 User Accounts
Change account type

 **Appearance and Per**

 Clock and Region
Change date, time, or nur

 Ease of Access
Let Windows suggest sett
Optimize visual display

2. Click on Network and Sharing Center".

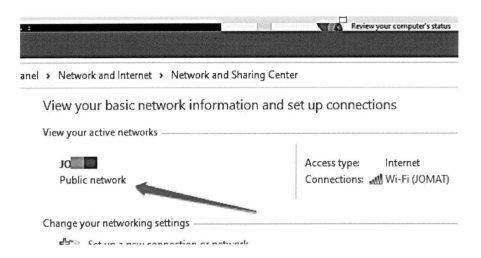

anel › Network and Internet › Network and Sharing Center

View your basic network information and set up connections

View your active networks

JO
Public network

Access type: Internet
Connections: Wi-Fi (JOMAT)

Change your networking settings

Set up a new connection or network

For your computer to join a Homegroup, it has to be a member of the same workgroup. The first time you join Homegroup, you will be required to enter your password. This process is only done once, subsequent joining won't require you entering your passwords.

How to share files on Windows 10

There are a variety of ways you can use to share your files or folders with other Windows users.

As a beginner, one method you will learn is how to share your files and folders using the share feature.

The share feature is inbuilt in Windows 10 File Explorer.

1. Open your system File Explorer.

2. Locate the file or folder you want to share and select.

3. Select files or folder and possibly multiples.

4. Click on the Share tab. And click on the Share button

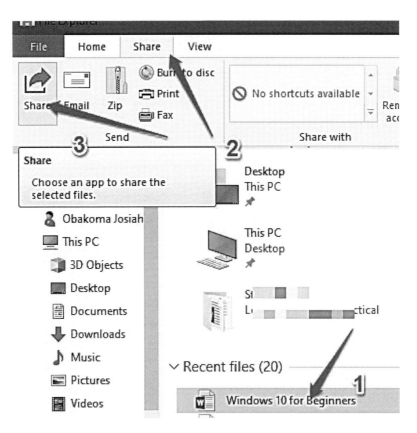

On the other hand, you can right-click the file or folder you want to share and click the on Share option in the context menu.

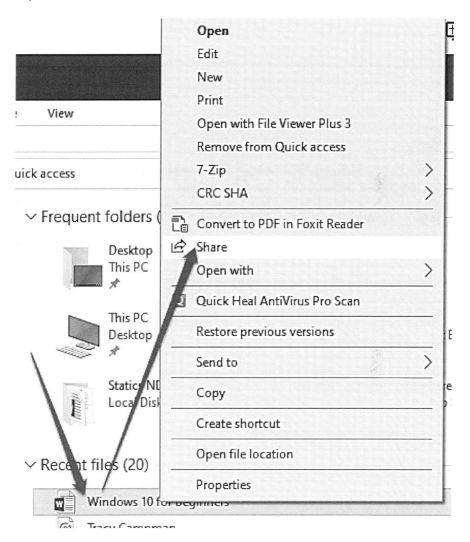

Follow the on-screen instruction to select or choose where or who you wish to share your document with.

Windows 10 Nearby File Sharing

Nearby sharing was first introduced in the April 2018 Windows 10 update version 1803. Nearby sharing allows Windows 10 users to transfer their files and connect their computers to a Nearby device using Wi-Fi or Bluetooth connection. If you are an Apple device user, Microsoft Windows 10 Nearby Sharing is similar to that of Apple's AirDrop. So you don't need and internet network or a USB flash drive to share that urgent file across.

How to Permit Nearby sharing on Windows 10

To enable Nearby sharing on your Windows 10 operating system;

1. Go to the *Settings app* on your Start Menu

2. Click on *System*.

3. Click on Shared experiences.

4. Toggle on Nearby Sharing

Manage your accounts

📲 Nearby sharing

Share content with a nearby device by using Bluetooth and Wi-Fi

⬤ On

I can share or receive content from

The same process is used to toggle Nearby sharing off. Another method to enable Nearby Sharing is through the Action Center on your Taskbar.

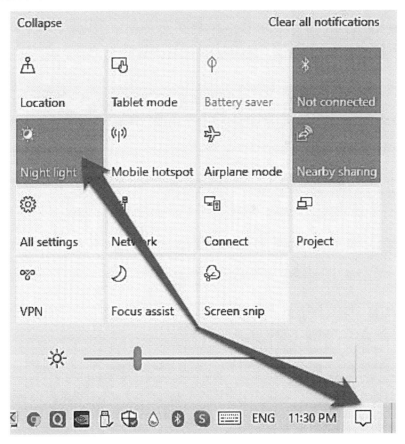

When enabled, you will have the button highlighted or sharded.

If the Nearby Sharing button is not available on your Action Center, you can quickly include it by

1. Going to the Settings App on your Start menu. Then click on System

2. Click on Notifications & actions, under "Quick actions," click on Edith your quick action

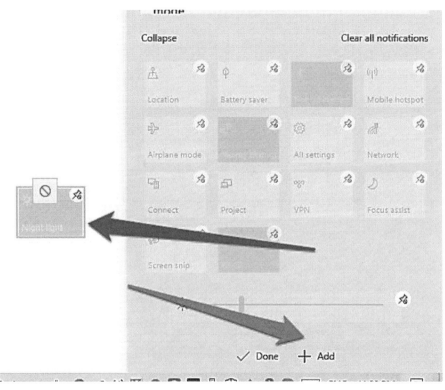

3. From the set of added quick actions, dragging any one of them out towards your left removes it from the list as shown above.

4. To add a button, click on Add and select from the list of actions you can add.

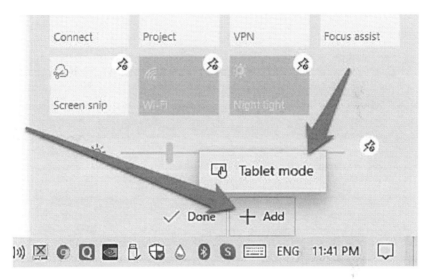

How to Change Windows 10 Nearby sharing settings

You can customize a few Nearby sharing settings possibly to control how you share and receive content.

1. Go to the Settings app on your Start Menu.

2. Click on *System* › *Shared experiences.*

3. Under "I can share or receive content from" click on the drop-down menu, and you're your selection:

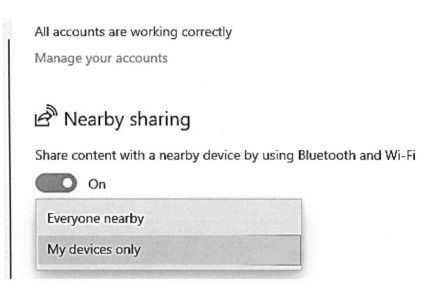

All accounts are working correctly

Manage your accounts

📡 Nearby sharing

Share content with a nearby device by using Bluetooth and Wi-Fi

⬤ On

Everyone nearby

My devices only

Everyone nearby – this option allows you to share and receive content from any nearby devices.

My devices only – this option restricts your computer to share and receive content only with devices using your Microsoft account.

By default, all transfers are stored in your "Downloads folder". If you choose to change it to a different folder, Under the "Save files I receive" option, click on the Change button. Next, select a location on your computer and click on Select Folder

Shared experiences

Share content with a nearby device by using Bluetooth and Wi-Fi

On

I can share or receive content from

My devices only

Save files I receive to

C:\Users\JOSIAH\Downlo...

Change

Transferring files using Nearby sharing

To transfer a file or folder using Nearby Sharing, always look out for the share button or icon.

To share your document, video, picture, or another type of file, through the File Explorer, right-click on the file and click on the share button.

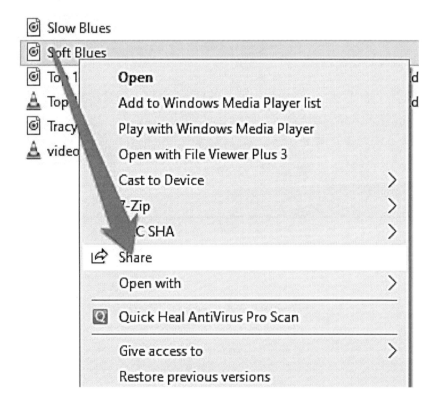

From the onscreen instructions, select the device from the list.

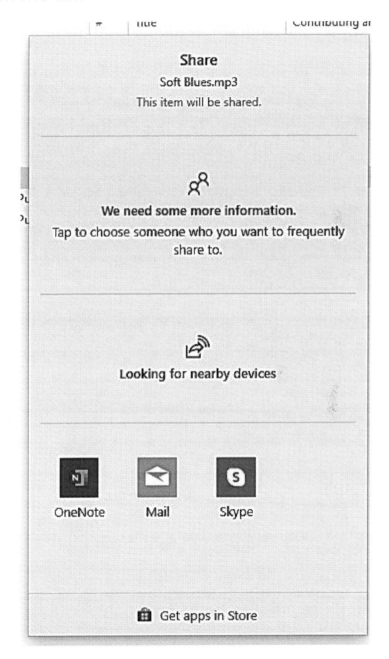

Chapter 8

Windows 10 Security

It is not that difficult to have your Windows 10 computer secured. What you need is to enable some basic security features of the Windows 10 operating system and disable some settings without putting your computer at risk.

Windows 10 Updates

To start up with, to ensure your Windows 10 computer is secured, you have to ensure you have the latest Windows updates.

Go to the search bar and enter "Check for updates"

Next click on the "Check for Updates" button to enable your computer search for any available updates using your internet connection.

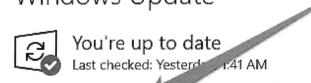

Windows Update

You're up to date
Last checked: Yesterd... 1:41 AM

Check for updates

This will ensure your system is secured from any lastest security threats.

Firewall and Network Protection

The Windows Defender Security Center is a Microsoft Windows application that provides a combined experience to view your computer status and control your security features, such as your firewall, antivirus and overall health of your computer. Having your Windows Defender Security Center active is not enough to safeguard your computer from malicious interference. You still need to activate your system firewall and antivirus.

To carryout check on your system Firewall settings, go to your search bar and enter "*Windows Security Settings*".

Click on the searched item. Once you are at the Windows Security settings, click on "Firewall & Network protection"

Windows Security

Windows Security is your home to view and manage the security and health of your device.

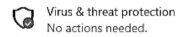

Protection areas

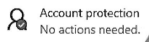

Virus & threat protection
No actions needed.

Account protection
No actions needed.

Firewall & network protection
No actions needed.

(ᵢₚ) Firewall & network protection

Who and what can access your networks.

Windows Community vi

Learn more about Firewall protection

Domain network

No action needed.

Have a question?

Get help

Private network

No action needed.

Who's protecting me?

Manage providers

Public network

No action needed.

Help improve Windows

Give us feedback

The word "No action needed" indicates my firewall is on either by my system antivirus of the Windows 10 Defence app.

Windows Defender Security Center. It's a good first step toward monitoring the overall health of your computer, but it's not going to be enough. One other layer of security is already built into Windows 10, and you should take advantage of it by enabling firewall and antivirus protection. Here's how:

Once enabled, transferring files and links with other devices is a very easy process with any application that includes the Windows 10 Share icon, such as Microsoft Edge, File Explorer, Photos, and many others.

How to Enable Automatic Updates

Having your Windows 10 PC set up to download and install updates automatically allows your PC to always have the latest security patches, performance, and stability improvements

To enable automatic Windows update

1. Open Settings.
2. Click on Update & Security.

i, microphone

Update & Security
Windows Update, recovery, backup

3. Click on Windows Update.
4. Click the Advanced options button.

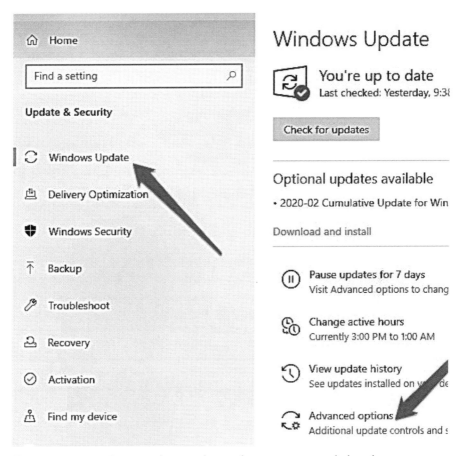

Ensure update downloads are enabled.

How to Add a New User Account to Windows 10

Creating a separate account on your PC will prevent other household users from having access to your files and apps. You have the ability to use the new Windows 10 cloud-based family settings feature on.

To add an Adult account to Windows 10 PC;

1. Go to Settings
2. Click on Accounts

ps
nstall, defaults, optional
tures

Accounts
Your accounts, email, sync
work, family

3. Click on *Your Family & other users.*
4. Under "Your Family" section, select Add a family member.

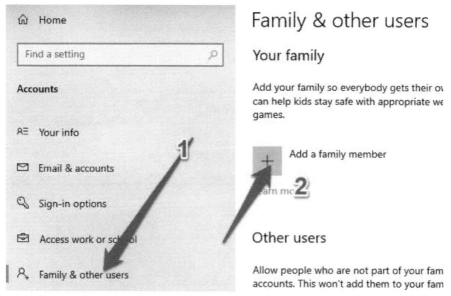

5. On the next screen, select Aaa and adult.

Microsoft

Add a child or an adult?

Enter the email address of the person you want to
add. If they use Windows, Office, Outlook.com,
OneDrive, Skype, or Xbox, enter the email address
they use to sign in.

○ Add a child

○ Add an adult

Enter their email address
_____

Cancel	Next

Click on the *Next* button and follow the onscreen
instructions to verify and complete the process.

Printed in Great Britain
by Amazon